Real Estate Salesmanship

Real Estate Salesmanship

"The Approaches"

**Thomas A. Jones,
CRS, GRI**

To order additional copies of this book, contact:
Xlibris Corporation
1-888-795-4274
www.Xlibris.com
Orders@Xlibris.com
77212

CONTENTS

*This book is dedicated to
two of my associates that have passed away:
Nat Moschini & Don Soja
& to all my associates that have worked with me
over the past thirty-eight years.*

INTRODUCTION

Tom obtained his real estate sales persons license in 1972 and was the first one to obtain the Million Dollar Sales Club award in Warren County, New Jersey in 1974. Tom obtained his broker's license in 1974, completed the GRI program, and achieved the CRS designation. He also taught the real estate license course for those wanting to enter the real estate business for thirty years. He is a past president of the Warren County Board of Realtors, presently serving on the Board of Directors, was a member of the Lopatcong Twp. School Board for seven years and served as President of that board for four years.

What Tom is most proud of is his family, his wife of fifty three years, his daughter, who works with him at the real estate office, his two sons, Steve in Florida, and Kevin in Georgia, and their families.

Tom has always believed in helping others meet their goals and giving help when he could and he is often called on for interpretations of real estate rules and ethical procedures in solving problems that may arise. He firmly believes that there is a right way of conducting the real estate business and it is the only way.

He prepared "THE APPROACHES" to help those starting out in the business and it might even help some who have been licensed for awhile. He hopes that the information will be helpful and his only wish is that everyone be successful and proud of what they are doing. What can be better than helping others accomplish their dreams in buying and selling and, as a result, we get paid!

Wishing you all good luck and with my best wishes.

Thomas A. Jones, CRS, GRI

CHAPTER 1

THE "ELM" APPROACH: EMPATHY, LISTENING AND MARKET

EMPATHY

The most important aspect of selling anything is the empathy you show to your clients and customers, it must be true empathy and honest. It will show itself and how it comes across will determine your degree of success. People want to deal with other people that show that they are truly interested in their well being and show their concern for them.

All of this builds up to the true designation of a professional.

When we talk about empathy, what are we really talking about? It's not the empty rhetoric that some people seem to have flow from them. It is the almost silent approach to hearing what the client or customer has to say and showing concern and acting accordingly with what is necessary to resolve their needs. It is that resolve and action that will prove true empathy and it's this action that will put you far above the crowd.

Be a professional, be concerned, and your future can be bright and successful.

LISTENING

Be a good listener. This is probably the second most important aspect of being a good real estate salesperson. Too many people are concerned about talking and not enough time listening. If we will only take the time to hear what the buyers and sellers are trying to say, we could make our job so much easier. Many times in talking with clients & customers and hearing what they are saying I can pick up information that will help me to show them the right properties and in talking with them, listening helps determine their motivations and other information that will be helpful in the selling them property or getting a listing.

In the initial conversation a buyer may say something like "I'm only interested in a basic home", but, in hearing them talk, we might pick up that what they really need or want is that formal dining room or family room, or that extra bathroom is really a necessity or that storage space is very important to them, making it necessary that there be a basement or storage area.

In the conversation you may pick up information that they have two cars and that a two car garage could be important, and it goes on from there.

What we are getting at here is the importance of listening because it is through listening that we can determine exactly what a purchaser is looking for which will help us reduce our work by narrowing down the number of homes that fit their needs. By the right approach it may only take a few showings in order to obtain an offer. When listening to the sellers, we can determine their motivation for selling, the time period they are looking at to move, whether there is flexibility in the pricing or terms of the sale, whether you can help them in purchasing the next home or refer them if they are moving out of State and it goes on from there.

MARKET

Know your market! By knowing what is available you can often picture a buyer in a particular house before even showing it to them. It may take awhile to acquire the knack of being able to do this but in a matter of time it can become routine. As a start, you should get to know what is available in your market area. Get to know the properties first hand, whether its by the caravan system or individual inspection. The better your knowledge of the properties the easier it is to sell.

In addition to knowing your market as far as housing is concerned, you should be familiar with the streets, roads, schools, churches, shopping, hospitals, restaurants and recreation areas in order to properly advise your buyer of these services, and, one the first things I like to do for someone new to the area is give them a tour before rushing out to show them houses. You will be surprised how much that approach is appreciated.

Be sure to know your utility services for your market area and be sure to advise the buyer and seller as early as possible about notification of change to the utilities prior to closing. This is very important to insure that there isn't any termination of services. Sellers should be requesting a final reading and the buyer should be calling for services starting on the same date, usually the date of closing.

SUMMARY

If we would follow these steps, it would help us to be more professional and it will help us to be an asset to those we serve.

THE "ELM" APPROACH

E-EMPATHY

L-LISTENING

M-MARKET

CHAPTER 2

THE "PAST" APPROACH: PROSPECTIING, ADVERTISEMENTS, SERVICING AND TIME

PROSPECTING

I find the best approach is the indirect approach because people do not generally like intrusions and want to enjoy their privacy but when you are talking to someone you can say something like "Mrs. Jones, I have people that have recently transferred to our area and they like the homes in your development, do you happen to know anyone that may be leaving your area that may be interested in selling their property?" Generally, you get at least a favorable reception, it's fresh, it doesn't come out to sound like "do you want to list your house?" which many have heard time after time and have caused many people to be apprehensive when a real estate salesperson makes contact with them. I believe that the indirect approach accomplishes the same results with very little adversity and, in fact, it often compliments you as a salesperson, and the office you are associated with. Remember, the act of prospecting, whether by phone or direct contact, should not end with the conversation but followed up with a "thank you" note and including your business card.

AD CALLS

The first contact with a buyer is often by the use of the telephone and many times it will be on an ad call. Be sure you know what is being advertised and where and be prepared to answer questions by having a copy of the listing information available but remember that the main purpose of the ad was to get the prospect to call, and you should have information on a few other comparable properties that are available in order to advise the buyer that you have more than just the home they called on. Never keep the buyer waiting on the telephone hold for any lengthy period of time because it becomes annoying to them. You also want to hear the buyer talk and if you need to collect your thoughts, ask the buyer to read the ad to you. Remember too that you are not a free information bureau, that is, you want that call to become a working prospect. Don't be afraid to ask for their name and phone number. I know that all of us realize that without that information we have nothing to work with. How many times have we heard "I just want to drive by". You should be able to come back with something like " I don't feel that you will be getting the true reflection of value on this one unless you see the inside as well. How about meeting me at 3:00PM or is 5:00PM better for you?" "I will show you the entire property, both inside & out and wait to you see what is in the back of the house!". "With the price of gas today I think it would be important for you see everything on one trip." In your conversation with the prospect you want to introduce yourself with the intent of getting their information, name, phone number, and address. If you are having some difficulty with getting information, don't be afraid of using something like "Mrs. Smith you don't seem interested in this particular property, we do have many others that may be of interest , can I have your name and address and I will forward information to you." They may also have an e-mail address, get that information and forward information to them.

It is important that your conversation not become antagonistic and so you should always make the conversation as pleasant as possible, even at the time of adversity, because how you handle a prospect on the phone can often make or break you. Be pleasant as possible, keep smiling, it helps!

SERVICING CLIENTS

How difficult is it to pick up and dial a number on the telephone? Not too difficult, right? Well then, how come so many property owners say something like "He took my listing and I never heard from him again." This really should never happen, but it does. It's bad for the salesperson's personal image and, on top of that, the image of the office that he or she is associated with and it goes on further by receiving statements like "those real estate sales people are no good!" and sometimes language that is even stronger. There is one thing for sure and that is if this practice continues it will demean our business and those associated with it. It is time to improve this by each of us doing our part. If we would only stay in touch with our sellers on a weekly basis or, at least, every ten days it would show them that you care and you are doing what you can to sell their property.

The telephone is a very intricate part of the follow up system, that is checking on mortgages and the process of them, obtaining additional deposits, getting inspections, checking details with attorney's, etc. It is also important that you are making notations about each contact and the information received from that source so that you have a running record of the process and that the information of importance is confirmed in writing. Don't leave things to chance because chances are something will go wrong and it sometimes happens that way. Cover yourself, put it in writing.

TIME

Use your time wisely and set aside a certain amount of time daily to do your calling and make it a part of your routine practice. It will help to make it a part of your daily life and will help towards your greater success.

SUMMARY

The use of the telephone and how you use it can help you to be a successful salesperson. Remember, that how you come across on the telephone is important, even if you have had a bad day, it's important to come over the telephone as cheerful and pleasant as possible. It takes practice but it is worth the effort. Try it and I think you will like the results.

THE "PAST" APPROACH

P-PROSPECTING

A-ADVERTISEMENTS

S-SERVICING

T-TIME

PAST

If we remember the

PAST

PRESENT

We can help the

Present

FUTURE

That will help to

Determine our future

CHAPTER 3

THE CCP APPROACH: CONTRACT COMPLETION PROCESS

CCP

When we finally get a buyer interested in a particular property and we have already spent a substantial amount of time with a buyer, we have to make sure that the contract is completed and presented as soon as possible but the first thing we want is to be sure of is that we have completed the contract form properly as this contract will become binding and enforceable, in some States after completion of attorney review. The information contained has to be complete and accurate so that there will be no headaches during the process.

NAMES & PROPERTY

First thing to do is make sure you have the proper names of the buyers and sellers, first name, middle initial, last name, Jr., Sr., etc. Secondly, make sure that you have the proper description of the property such as the correct Block number and Lot number. Don't take the listing form information alone as being correct, but double check with the tax reference information or, if it is your listing, you may have a copy of the tax bill, deed, or survey. Generally, it will show the size of the property. This is another important area to check because you want to be sure what the buyer is getting because, if it isn't, the buyer may negate the contract. Don't leave anything to chance, get it right!

DEPOSIT MONIES

The area of deposit monies is very important. You want to obtain as much of an initial deposit you can with the balance of 5% to 10% within five to ten days, in States that require contracts drawn by real estate agents being accepted by the attorneys for the buyers & sellers allow sufficient time for completion of the attorney review. In the event you have a low down payment or no down payment buyer, you want a deposit that will cover the buyers closing costs and mark the agreement accordingly. Make sure that you diary for the additional deposit so that the buyer will be in compliance with the agreement.

Balance of down payment (if any) should be indicated and after all the figures are in double check to make sure that they ad up, the top number and bottom number should be equal.

MORTGAGE

Be sure to indicate the type of mortgage that the buyer is going to obtain and the number of years of that mortgage. Where you specify an interest rate, the term "current" or "prevailing" should be utilized due to changes in mortgage rates; however, you should specify a maximum rate based on the qualifications of your buyer. Be sure to give yourself adequate time for obtaining the mortgage, that is, thirty to forty-five days for conventional financing and slightly more for VA or FHA financing.

CLOSING

It should be indicated the type of deed to be conveyed, the balance of the down payment at time of closing and the approximate closing date. Make sure that the closing date has some reference to the time to obtain the mortgage, for instance, if you give forty-five days for a mortgage commitment, you need the closing date 15 to 30 days after that date. The time element may vary from area to area , depending on the amount of time it takes to get everything clear to close but the important thing is to allow enough time so that problems are not created.

TENANTS

If the property is presently rented, be sure to indicate the name of the tenant, how much rent they are paying (as well as deposit) and the terms of the lease, month to month, one year, etc. If it is the intent of the buyer to occupy the property and they want the tenant out it should be indicated in the agreement who is responsible for having the property vacated.

INCLUDED IN SALE

Most contracts have standard information on what remains with the property upon closing but many items included in the listing as remaining are often forgotten as being mentioned in the contract. If the listing form shows that the refrigerator stays, or the lawn mower, or patio furniture, or fireplace equipment, or above ground pool & equipment, etc, be sure to indicate these items in the contract. Under the parol evidence rule, the contract is the last negotiable agreement and what was in the listing may not stand

EXCLUDED FROM SALE

If there are specific items which would normally be considered as fixtures that are being removed, be sure to indicate the item that is being removed, replaced, or exchanged.

INSPECTIONS

In view of the amount of litigations as respects problems with infestations and structural problems, it is recommended that inspections be obtained, usually by the buyer, and that the purchase is subject to satisfactory inspections being obtained or the buyer may cancel the agreement. Often time problems can be resolved by negotiations, that is, the seller will often agree to either repair what is necessary or agree to a price adjustment and have the buyer resolve the problem. It should be noted that an inspector will be looking at the structure mechanical makeup, and infestation, not just termites but any form of infestation, insects and vermin.

Country homes may require septic/cesspool and well inspections which would fall within the definition of a home inspection and usually conducted by the same inspection company and, again, if there is a problem the buyer has the right to terminate the agreement. Be careful not to assume that the property has a septic system, if it is an older home it may still have a cesspool. Well water may be from a deep well or shallow and in some cases, spring fed. Careful examination should be taken to make sure that there are no problems; however, if there are problems, hopefully they can be resolved.

Home inspection reports are common with many purchases, including transferees with their employer requiring that the inspections be done. Our position is to recommend that the buyer obtain inspections by a reputable inspection company to be sure that there are no immediate problems with the structure. This also protects the seller from any possible litigation, unless they were aware of the problem and didn't disclose it. The buyer has the right to waive such inspections if they so desire.

Things to watch out for: "the property has a septic system" and it turns out to be cesspool. "The property has city water" and it turns out that it has a well. "it has a well" and it turns out that there is no well, it has a cistern. Watch out for statements that you can not substantiate. When you are not sure just advise that their inspection should show or confirm what the property has and doesn't have.

GENERAL INFORMATION

You will want to have the addresses, telephone numbers, on all the parties to the contract, that is, the buyer, seller, attorneys, and real estate agents. This information, of course, will be helpful to you in the process and conclusion of the transaction. When it comes to attorney's and inspection companies, you should give your client a choice of two or three names, allow them to select who they want to use. If you recommend one attorney or one inspection company and there is a problem it will become your problem.

COMMISSION

This is what we are looking forward to and we want to make sure it is properly spelled out in the contract. If it is another broker's listing just spell out your commission as stated in the listing. The listing agent is covered by their listing agreement.

SUMMARY

This is basically an overview and it does not cover every aspect or contingency that may occur, but the important thing is to make each and everyone of us to think before we act and hopefully what we do will be to the best of our ability with the protection and satisfaction of all the parties to the contract. Some will say, "why should I recommend inspections" I would reply, "that in order to protect the buyer and seller from any adversity, isn't it better that those inspections be done and doesn't it help protect them from legalities and ourselves as well?." I believe that it does.

When we are drawing contracts or offers, if we try a little harder, I believe we can improve our lot and our image, and it's up to each one of us to do our best in this area and we owe it to those we serve.

THE CCP APPROACH

C-CONTRACT

C-COMPLETION

P-PROCESS

CHAPTER 4

THE LCP APPROACH: LISTING COMPLETION PROCESS

LCP

I'm basically going to cover the process of the listing format here with the hope that some of this information will be helpful. It is annoying to see the variations of the same basic forms and too many times incorrect or incomplete information, yet this is one of the most important functions, if not the most important, because it is from this information that we make our sales. This is an area that basically should be reviewed very carefully to make sure the listing form is complete and accurate and that the sellers intent is expressed in the form itself, that is , the seller is totally aware of what they are selling and what price and they know what is included in the sale of the property and what is not.

STREET ADDRESS

It shouldn't be too difficult but how many times have I found the house numbers reversed or even totally wrong. It may show the mailing address which included the postal area but doesn't show the actual location, such as the township the property is actually located in, and, on occasion, the township is shown and it's the wrong one! If we are starting off bad here, you can imagine the balance of the form and what we are going to wind up with. Let's get it right!

LOT, BLOCK, OR TAX MAP

What we have to do here is make sure we have the right sequence of numbers and that we haven't reversed the numbers. If the property is being sub-divided, be sure to indicate that the sale is only part of such and such, unless a new number has already been assigned to the new lot.

LOT SIZE

This area is very important due to the fact that if its not accurate, the buyer may wind up walking away without any obligations. Be sure to check your reference material as to the accuracy of the size of the property as it is described on the listing form. If possible, check to see if a survey map is available, or check the dimensions as described in the deed.

TAX INFORMATION

We often see "taxes about $1,400" and we later find out its twice that amount. Let's be factual about this and publish the correct, current tax for the property. You can either check with the owner with them supplying a copy of the tax bill or checking with the tax reference material to determine the assessment times the current tax rate. Be careful when using copies of tax bills that you disregard the discounts such senior citizens and veteran's, and publish the actual tax rate figures. You should also indicate the year that the tax applies to. I have found this area to be of a particular problem over the years because buyers think they are getting a low tax situation but in actuality they are not. It is very important that we get this right so that we don't get into an area of misrepresentation.

OWNER INFORMATION

If the listing is being published by a multiple listing service, cooperating brokers may be getting offers and you want them to be as accurate as possible in completing their offer/contract form and it would be very helpful if the legal names of the owners appeared on the listing form, that is, the first name, middle initial, last name, Jr., Sr., etc. and all that have an ownership interest in the property be indicated.

The directions for the showing of the property should be indicated on the listing, whether all showings require the contact with the listing broker or can they call the owner direct, and, if they can, the telephone number for contact. If there are any telephone numbers indicated double check and make sure that they are correct.

SERVICES

Is there city water and sewers and are they actually hooked up to the system? Don't take anything for granted, you can be surprised! Is it possible that there may be a septic or cesspool? There is a difference and you have to be sure that the correct one is indicated. Is there a well or spring fed water system? Be sure to ask the sellers specifically about this so that the listing form is properly filled out. If there is a well and the owner is aware of the depth of it, it could be noted in the listing.

Be sure to indicate the correct type of heating system and how its heat is supplied. If it's oil, how large is the tank & where is it located (in the basement or in ground). The electric system, is it a fuse system or circuit breakers and what is the amperes.

NON FIXTURES

If the seller is going to leave items like the refrigerator, washer, dryer, above ground pool & equipment, fireplace equipment, drapes, curtains, area rugs, etc. be sure to indicate the items being left with the property and be sure to go over this list with the sellers so that they are fully aware that these items remain with the house upon closing of the property.

DESCRIPTION

You want to describe the property to bring out the highlights but don't get carried away as you don't want disappointed buyers showing up at the door. Always describe the positive points first and if there any negative points save them to the end.

SUMMARY

This will give you a basic area of information for consideration when doing listings; however, I haven't covered everything. When in doubt, check it out! I hope that this will help in having more accurate listings and less headaches.

THE LCP APPROACH

L-LISTING

C-COMPLETION

P-PROCESS

CHAPTER 5

THE ACE APPROACH:
AVOIDING COMMON ERRORS

ACE

What we have to do is provide the best possible professional service that we can provide and the one principle way of providing that service is to know what we are talking about, and, in our case, the real estate business. The more education we have in the area of real estate services, the better we can perform. I'm not saying that the education has to be all classroom or formal type of learning but we can also learn by doing and asking questions and getting answers. It's almost like a constant learning process for those successful in real estate and in order to maintain that success they must continue to be active, willing to learn and continue to maintain the one outstanding necessity for continued success in real estate and that is EMPATHY. Without that main ingredient there cannot be real success.

The area that I want to cover here is avoiding common errors with the hope that this information can be of help to others in avoiding certain common mistakes, some of which the writer over the years has been caught up in.

SHOWING PROPERTY

One of the most common mistakes as I see it, that is often made is the treating of showing properties like a sightseeing tour. We, of course, are not in the tour business but in the business of selling properties. I'm not saying that you shouldn't show the buyers the area so that they can become familiar with the attributes of the community, but in the number of homes that are being shown. In order to be successful you have to be able to control what is happening, at least to the best of your ability. If you have qualified your buyer and know what they want, you should be able to come up with five or six properties that fit the buyers direction or needs as to the type of properties they desire and try to limit the number of showings in order that the buyers can retain some of the details of the properties you are showing them. Showing them too many properties will only get them confused and lost, they won't be able to remember what they have been shown.

Some salespersons insist on talking right through the showings. How can the buyers retain anything of what you are suppose to be showing them if they are too much involved in conversation? Let the buyer SEE and don't get into statements like "this is the living room", "this is the kitchen", etc. It's already quite obvious what these rooms are. If you want, point out some of the extra plus features about the property that may not be obvious, like the extra insulation in the attic, the central air-conditioning system, or the refrigerator, washer, dryer, etc that remain with the property. Keep the conversation short, let the buyers look and observe. I once had a seller call me up to complain about a salesperson showing her property. She said "he didn't say anything while he was showing the property." I said that he was a good agent, he discussed the property before the showing and asked for comments after the showing, he was a good agent.

Conversation with the sellers should be avoided if at all possible. If your buyers have questions, advise them something like "the questions you have raised are very good points to check out, I'll discuss them with the listing agent and let you know." This gives you the opportunity for a follow up after the showing with additional information with the hope of getting the offer. Remember too, that this business revolves around time, that is, if you don't do it right away, the property may no longer be available.

If you are making statements about the property, area, schools, or whatever, make sure you know what you are talking about, don't guess or assume anything. If you don't know the answers, get them and make sure that they are accurate. You can make or break yourself, and your future, by how you handle yourself in this area. Why not do it right from the beginning, what follows becomes easier.

In showing a home that you assume no one is home, I have had a lot of surprises here, including the first year I was in this business when I threw open the door to the bathroom and found it occupied, and another time having thought the house was vacant and having the owner running down the stairs with his dog right behind him, and another time when I called the property owner several times, no answer, went to the property and opened up the master bedroom and found the woman home in bed. Be sure, call first, knock, ring the doorbell, open the door and holler "anyone home". Who needs surprises!

Properties should be left the way you found them. Turn the lights off and check the door to make sure it's locked and double check yourself before leaving the premises. If your prospective buyer has flushed the toilet, make sure that it has stopped after filling and check the faucets and make sure they are also turned off, etc. These seem like very simple things but you would be surprised the number of times I have received calls about salespersons leaving this on or that, or owners coming home and finding the door unlocked. We certainly don't want sellers angry about us leaving the property with the lights on or doors unlocked and we want to retain a good relationship with them, after all, its from these properties that we make a living. Lets respect their investment as we hope others would respect ours, and treat the property like it were your own.

LISTING INFORMATION

Even though we find the information to be helpful in determining the properties we want to show our prospective buyers, we should not accept everything on the listing form as being totally accurate. One area that is often found incorrect is the tax information, recheck this area using your own source material. Sometimes we find the tax information shown is from last year and should be checked to make sure that you have the current tax data.

Lot size information is another area that people (sellers) may say something like "it's a half acre lot", and the inexperienced salesperson puts it down that way, but it turns out that the lot is only a quarter of an acre. If you sold this property with the assumption that it had a ½ acre lot and it turns out that it isn't, who do you think the buyer is going to blame? Besides this it may cost the transaction. Double check lot size!

When it comes to utility expenses, I find it better not to quote figures unless I know exactly what these costs are. Also, every person or family has a different life style and the utility costs for one may not be that for another. This is an area that you should use caution in making claims about how low the heating costs are, especially when you know that the present owners are never home or other similar circumstances.

SUMMARY

All we have to remember is to know the truth, express the truth, and you will start building your future from day one. Don't try to be something you are not, be yourself, be proud of what you are doing, be understanding, treat others the way you would like to be treated, be knowledgeable, be a participant in a learning program, be active in your office and your Realtor association, be active in your community, but most importantly, be active with your own family because you will need their support in order to have any degree of success.

THE ACE APPROACH

A-AVOIDING

C-COMMON

E-ERRORS

CHAPTER 6

THE SAFETY APPROACH: AVOIDING HAZARDS

When we first obtain our real estate license we are anxious to make our first sale or obtain our first listing but we might be in too big of a hurry. You have to use caution to make sure that you are working under safe circumstances.

When you are working with a buyer try to get them into the office and try to obtain a pre-qualification letter from them, either from their bank or two or three suggestions you may have. DO NOT be in a hurry to meet someone at a listed property as they may not be qualified to buy it and, if it's vacant, it may be a set up. By getting them into the office first allows you to get the qualification and, if they are up to no good, they will not normally come into an office.

In getting calls for listing properties for sale, be sure that you are dealing with the owner of the property, run a tax search to confirm ownership and to confirm taxes and dimensions of the property. There was a case that a listing was signed by one of the owners but not the other and when it came to close, it didn't, because the other side did not agree to the sale. They were in the process of getting divorced but it wasn't final yet and one of the questions that might be asked, "does anyone else have a financial interest in this property?" Often times when the property was purchased, the party buying the property may have been single at the time but has since married. You want to make sure that everyone that has an interest in the property is signing the listing agreement and they would all have to sign the contract of sale as well.

When doing "OPEN HOUSE" sales, the men normally don't have a problem here but the woman sometimes are targets and should take all precautions, especially in vacant houses, by having a friend or family member be with you, it is not worth the risk to be alone, especially in these times when there are so many bad things happening. Play it safe!

The real estate business is still one of the best professions you can have and it can be successful if you are patient with it, work on letting the world know that you have a real estate license and you are ready to help people meet their goals of buying or selling.

QUALIFICATIONS

THOMAS A. JONES, CRS, GRI
REALTOR / BROKER

1) LICENSED REAL ESTATE BROKER & RESIDENTIAL APPRAISER IN THE STATES OF NEW JERSEY & PENNSYLVANIA.

2) THIRTY-EIGHT YEARS OF EXPERIENCE IN RESIDENTIAL, COMMERCIAL, INDUSTRIAL, & LAND SALES, LISTINGS, AND RESIDENTIAL APPRAISALS.

3) COMPLETED REAL ESTATE SALESPERSONS COURSE & APPRAISAL COURSES AT THE PROFESSIONAL SCHOOL OF BUSINESS.

4) COMPLETED REAL ESTATE BROKERS COURSE AT MORRIS COUNTY COMMUNITY COLLEGE.

5) MEMBER OF WARREN COUNTY AND LEHIGH VALLEY BOARD OF REALTORS & THEIR MULTIPLE LISTING SERVICES.

6) MEMBER OF THE NATIONAL ASSOCIATION OF REALTORS.

7) LICENSED REAL ESTATE INSTRUCTOR, APPROVED BY THE NEW JERSEY REAL ESTATE

COMMISSION & HAVE TAUGHT REAL ESTATE
CLASSES SINCE 1980.

8) CERTIFIED REAL ESTATE APPRAISER (CREA),
FOR THE NATIONAL ASSOCIAION OF REAL
ESTATE APPRAISERS.

9) MEMBER OF THE NEW JERSEY ASSOCIATION
OF REALTORS MILLION DOLLAR CLUB FOR
SEVERAL YEARS AND THE FIRST ONE TO
ACHIEVE THAT AWARD FROM WARREN
COUNTY IN 1974 AND THE SECOND ONE TO
ACHIEVE THE "GOLD" AWARD IN 1987.

10) GRADUATE OF THE NEW JERSEY ASSOCIATION
OF REALTORS SPONSORED GRADUATE
REALTOR INSTITUTE GRI PROGRAM IN
1984.

11) ACHIEVED THE NATIONAL ASSOCIATION
OF REALTORS MARKETING INSTITUTE
CERTIFIED RESIDENTIAL SPECIALISTS, CRS
DESIGNATION IN 1988.

12) MEMBER OF THE NATIONAL ASSOCIATION
OF REALTORS REAL ESTATE APPRAISAL
SECTION (FOUNDING MEMBER)